2359

7365

YOUR TEETH

Joan Iveson-Iveson

Illustrated by Bill Donohoe

The Bookwright Press
New York · 1985

All About You

Your Eyes
Your Teeth

Acknowledgments

All the photographs in this book were supplied by Sally and Richard Greenhill, with the exception of the following: Jim Merrett 16, 20.

First published in the United States in 1985 by
The Bookwright Press
387 Park Avenue South
New York, NY 10016

First published in 1985 by
Wayland (Publishers) Limited
49 Lansdowne Place, Hove,
East Sussex BN3 1HF, England
© 1985 Wayland (Publishers) Limited

ISBN 0-531-18013-1
Library of Congress Catalog Card Number: 84-73573

Printed by G. Canale & C.S.p.A., Turin, Italy

Contents

What are teeth for?	4
Baby teeth	6
Adult teeth	8
What are teeth made of?	10
The work they do	12
Why teeth decay	14
Cleaning your teeth	16
Visiting the dentist	20
Looking after your teeth	22
Word list and Index	24

What are teeth for?

Your teeth are very important. Without them you couldn't eat all the things you enjoy, like a nice juicy hamburger, or a crunchy apple. With **gums** alone, you would be like a baby, living on liquids and mashed-up foods.

Not everybody's teeth look the same. Some people have big teeth, others have small or crooked teeth, or teeth with gaps. Teeth are not always white, sometimes they are nearly yellow.

Sharks grow new teeth all the time, but you cannot do that. Your teeth must last a lifetime. To look after them properly you should first find out all about them.

Baby teeth

You will have two sets of teeth in your lifetime. The first set are called "milk" or "baby" teeth. Their real name is deciduous teeth. A deciduous tree loses its leaves in autumn, and these first teeth will also be lost later on.

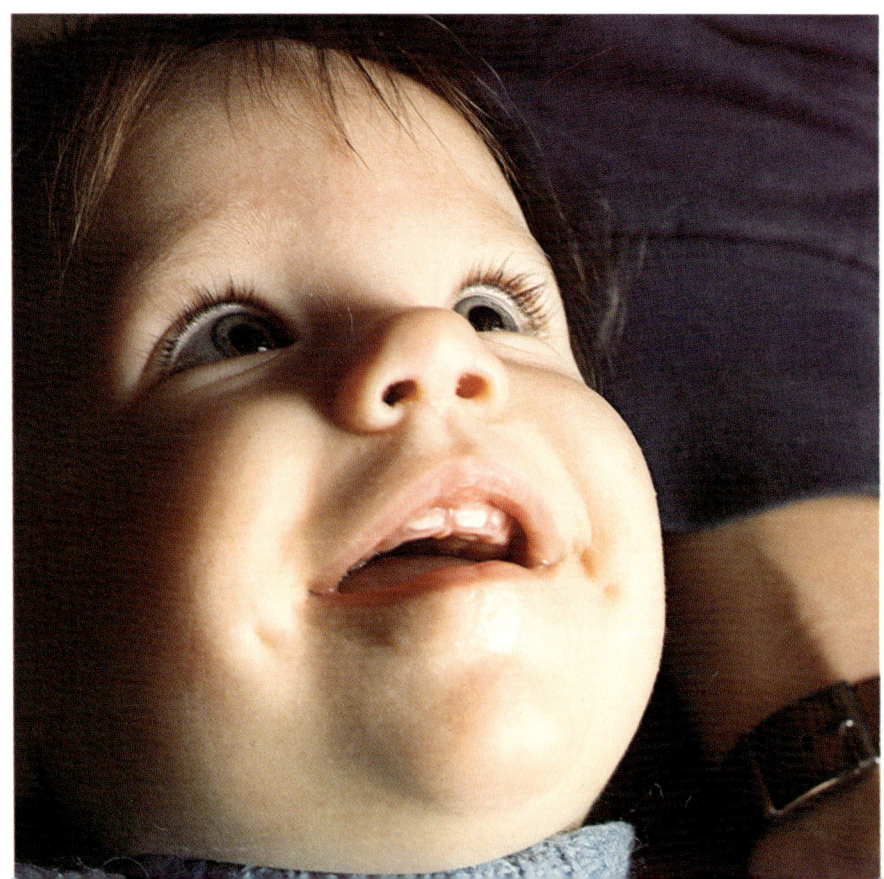

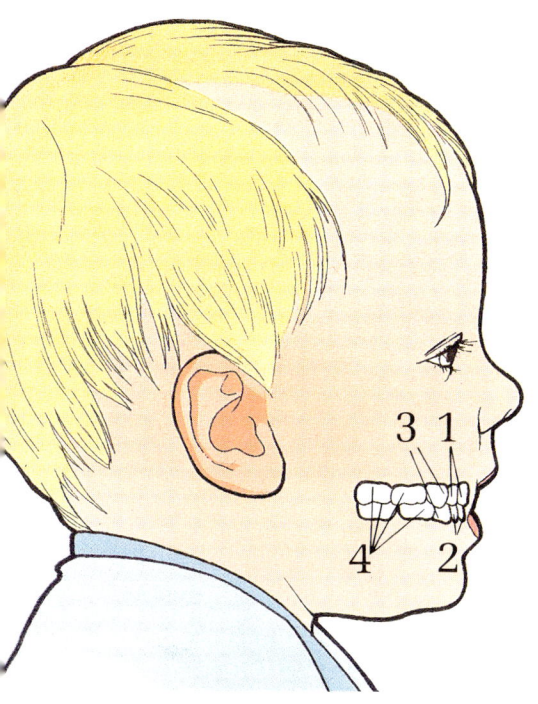

A baby's teeth

1 incisor
2 incisor
3 canine
4 molar

There are 20 of them and they have different names. They begin to appear when you are about 6 months old. Until then they are hidden away inside the jawbones. They push through the gums, two at a time. This is called **teething**. By the time a baby is 18 months old it may have nearly all its first teeth.

Teething can be painful and a baby is given hard things to bite and chew on to help the teeth come through.

Adult teeth

You do not keep your baby teeth. They first begin to grow loose and fall out when you are about 6. Hidden away in the gums are the adult, or permanent teeth. Because you are growing all the time there is more room in your mouth, and you will have 32 adult teeth. The last of them will come through when you are about 21.

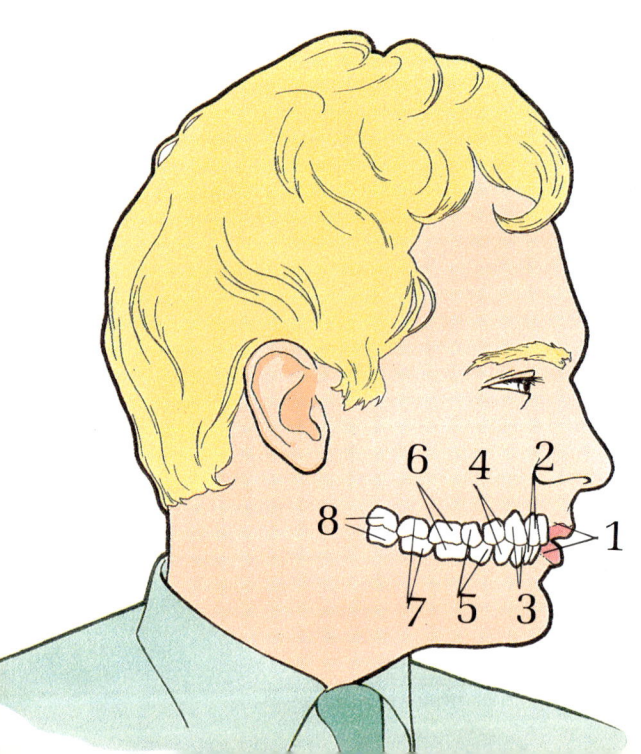

An adult's teeth

1 incisor
2 incisor
3 canine
4 premolar
5 premolar
6 molar
7 molar
8 wisdom tooth

The first baby teeth to come out are the front teeth. Teeth have always been thought of as having magic. Many children put a lost tooth under the pillow at night, hoping the tooth fairy will take it and leave some money behind.

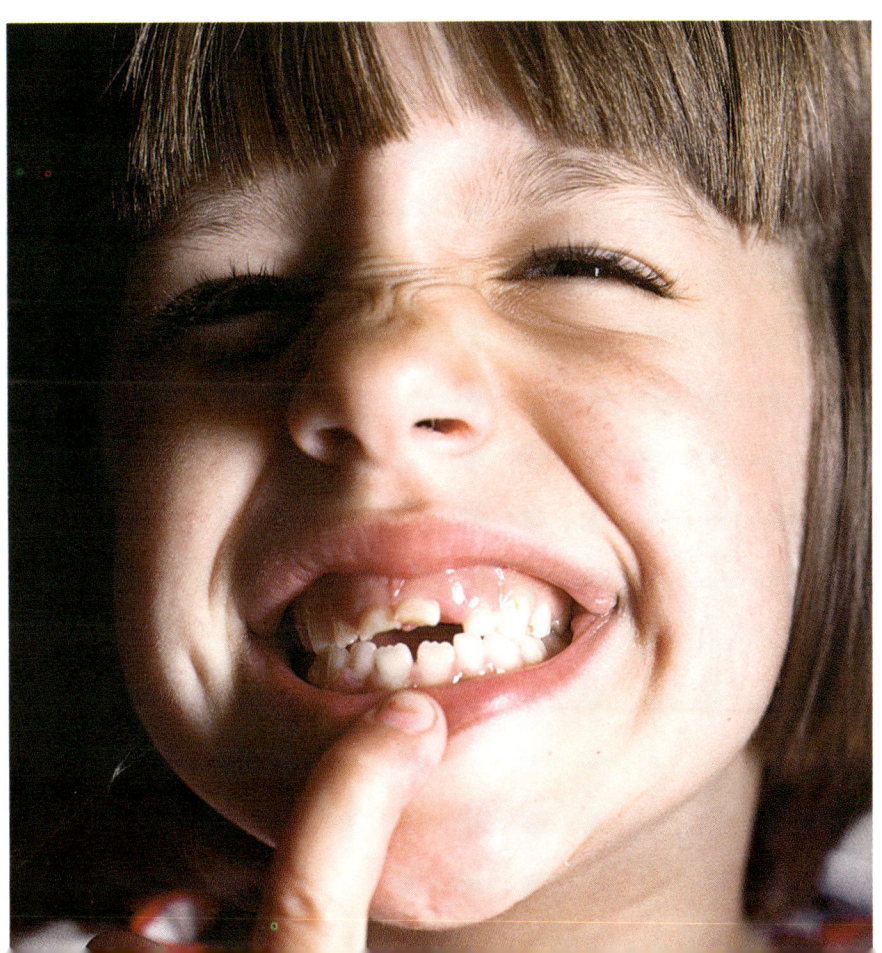

What are teeth made of?

Your teeth fit into sockets or holes, in your jawbones. The sockets are covered on the outside by your gums. The teeth can move very slightly inside the sockets. This means they will not be damaged if you bite on something like a very hard candy.

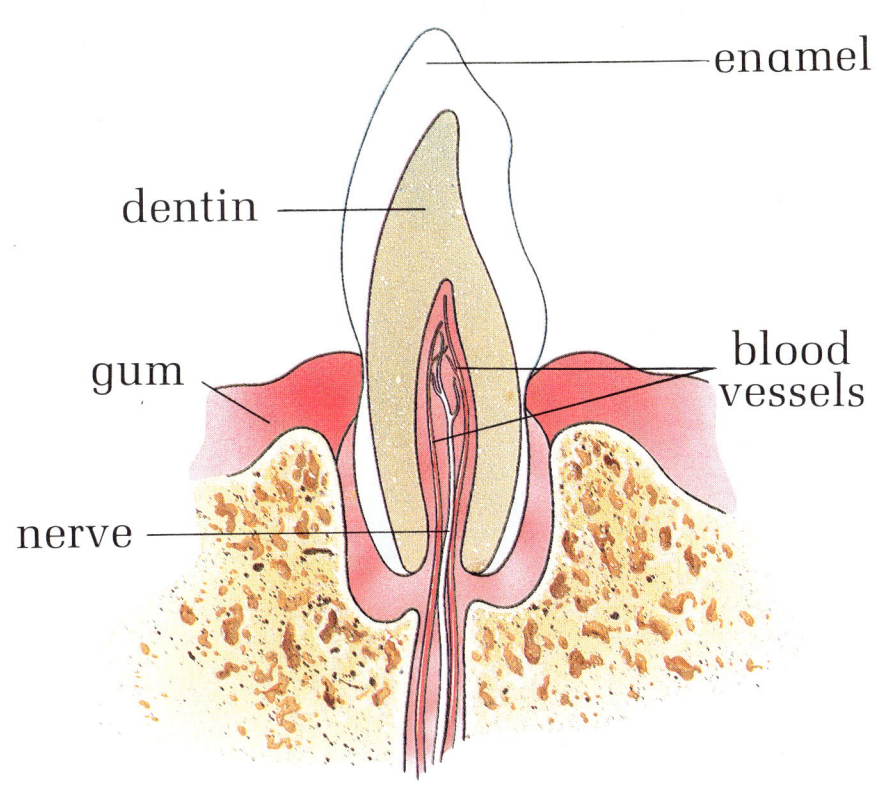

This drawing looks right inside a tooth. The outside is made of **enamel,** the hardest material in your body. Underneath is **dentin**, which is like bone. In the center is the soft part where the **nerves** and **blood vessels** are. The blood keeps the tooth alive, and the nerves send messages to the brain and also get information from it. Your nerves tell your brain when you have toothache.

The work they do

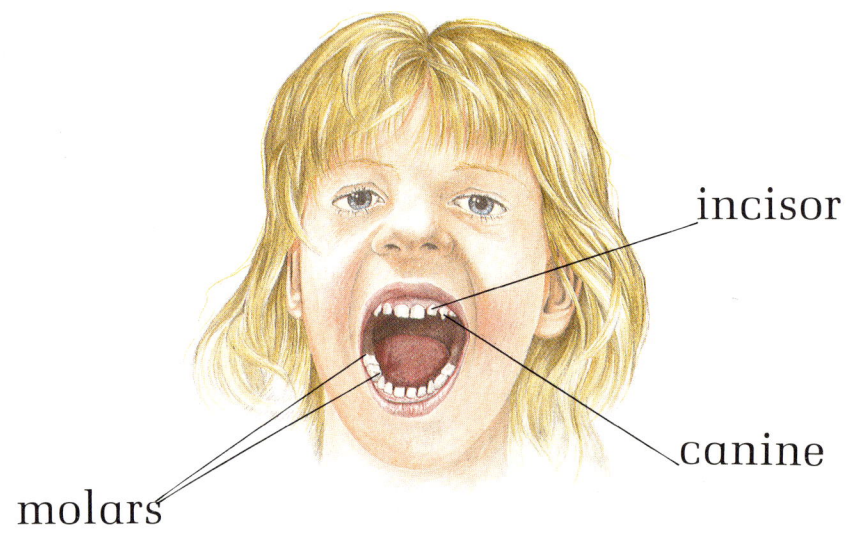

Your teeth are not all the same shape and size. Different teeth have different jobs to do when they chew up your food. If you look at the drawing you can see the different teeth. The **incisors**, or front teeth, and **canines** are sharp, and cut and tear your food. The **molars** are flatter and bumpy, and they grind up your food so that you can swallow it easily.

When you are eating, your teeth all work together to mash your food up into smaller and smaller pieces, and mix it with spit. Saliva is the correct name for this watery liquid you can feel in your mouth. It helps soften the food so you can swallow it easily. Saliva helps keep your mouth clean and also helps you to talk. Sometimes you cannot speak when you are frightened because the saliva dries up.

Why teeth decay

Animals nearly always keep their teeth all their lives. People are not so lucky. Can you think why? It has to do with what you eat and drink. Unlike animals, most people like to eat lots of sweet, sugary foods. Sugar is bad for your teeth and causes holes to form. This is called tooth decay.

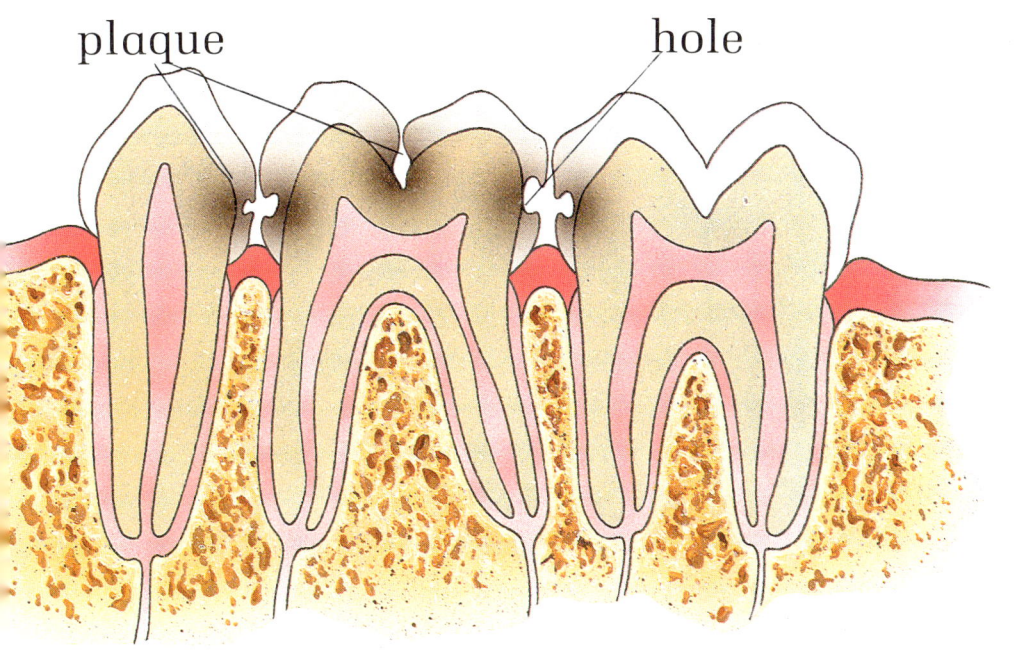

This drawing shows where tooth decay has happened. Tiny germs, called bacteria, live in your mouth and feed on the sugar you eat. This makes a sticky stuff called **plaque** which clings to your teeth. Plaque attacks the hard outsides of your teeth and begins to make tiny holes, or cavities. The cavities will not mend by themselves. After a while they will get bigger and bigger. Only the dentist can stop the damage.

Cleaning your teeth

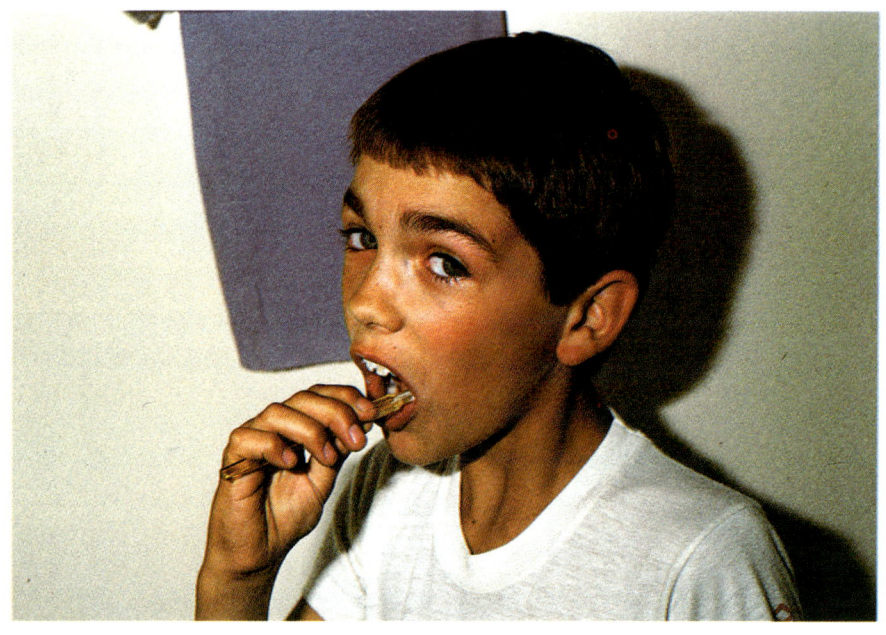

Do you always clean your teeth properly? You should brush them twice a day – after breakfast and at bedtime. You need your own toothbrush with a small head and soft nylon bristles. If you can, you should buy a new one every month. You must never let anyone else use it.

Choose toothpaste which has **fluoride** in it. Fluoride strengthens the hard enamel on the outsides of your teeth. You can also buy fluoride mouthwash. Lastly, you can use disclosing tablets. These stain your teeth red in the places where there is plaque, the sticky stuff that makes holes in your teeth.

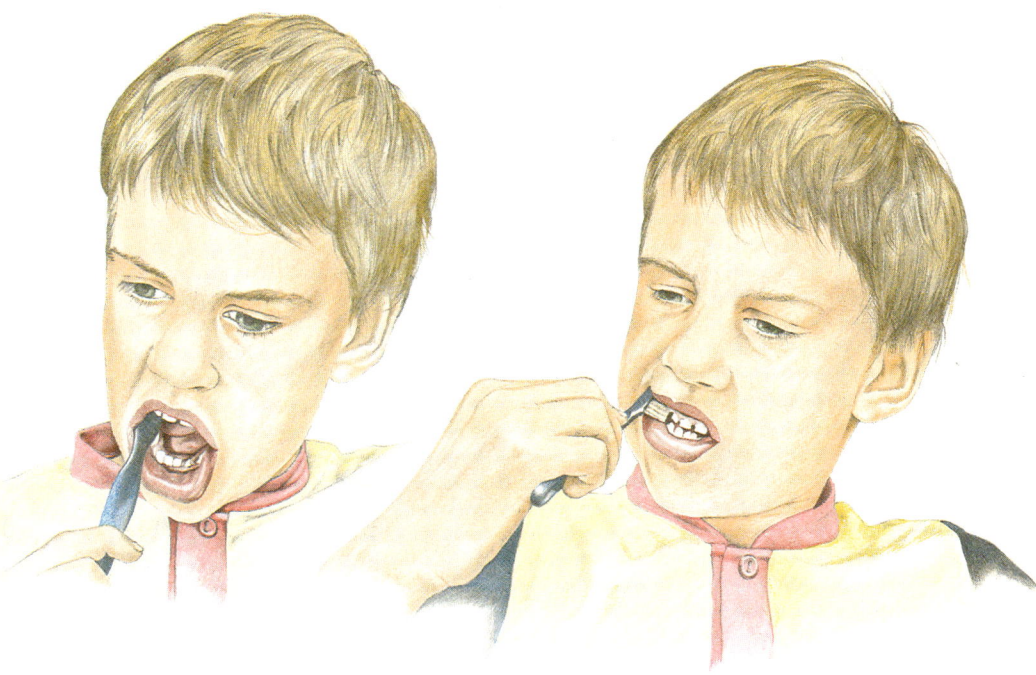

When you are ready to brush your teeth, make sure you have a good light to see by and a big mirror in front of you. Get your mouthwash and discloser ready and then squeeze some toothpaste onto your brush. Begin with your teeth together. Hold the brush so all the bristles are against your teeth. Start brushing around the outsides of your teeth.

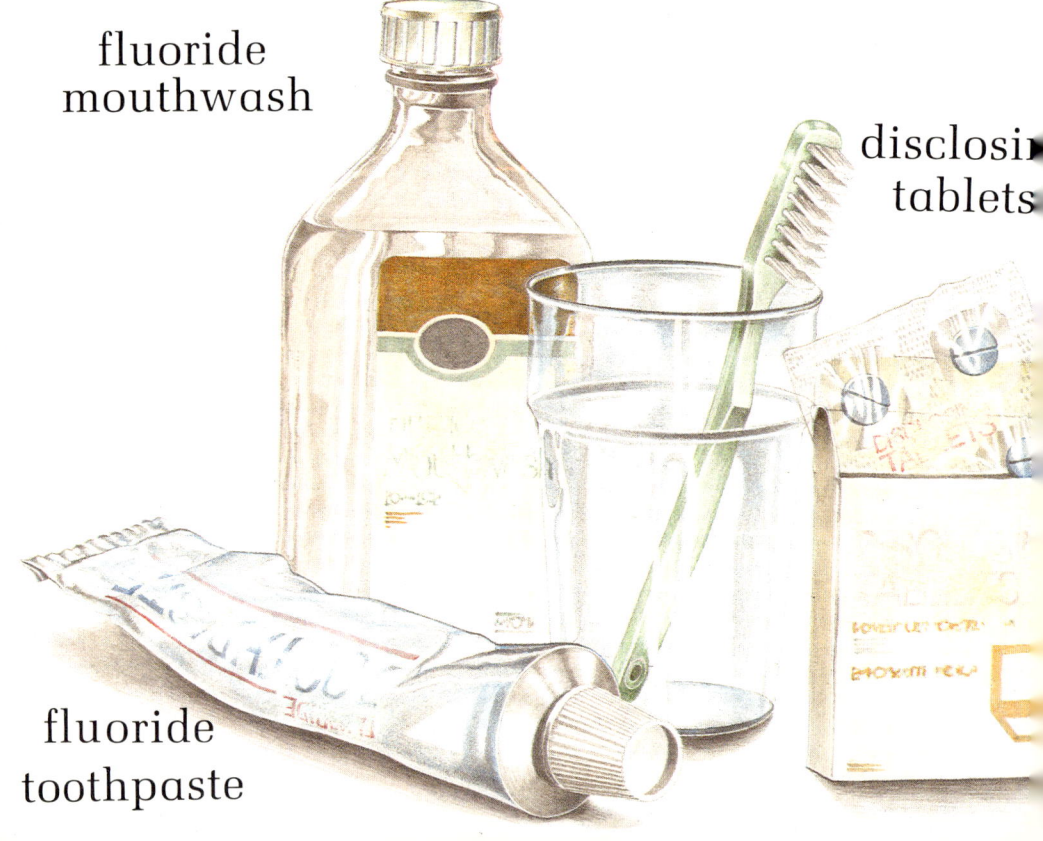

fluoride mouthwash

disclosing tablets

fluoride toothpaste

Move your toothbrush around and around in small circles. Then open your mouth and brush the insides of your teeth. Last, brush the biting and chewing surfaces. Doing this correctly takes five minutes. Now use the mouthwash and rinse carefully. Last use a disclosing tablet, if you like. If there are any red stains left after rinsing your mouth, you must brush your teeth again!

Visiting the dentist

Your dentist looks after your teeth, and checks them carefully with special instruments. An **x ray** might be taken to look right inside your jaw. A dentist will tell you the best way to clean your teeth, and what foods are good and bad for them. If your teeth are not growing

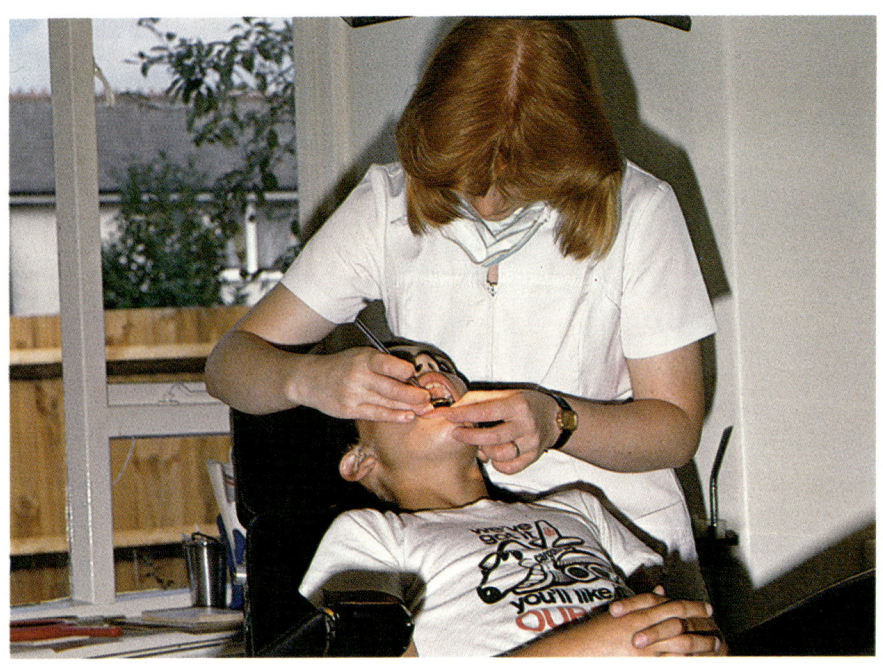

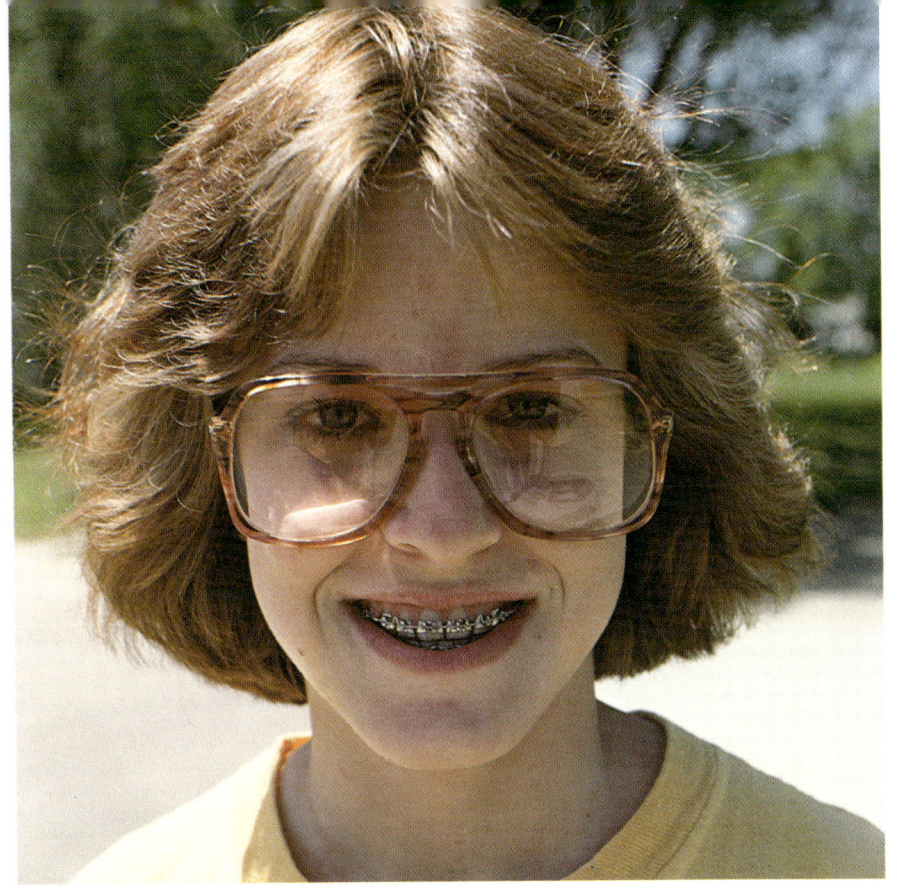

straight you may need special wire **braces** fitted for a while. Sometimes you will need a **filling** to mend a hole in your tooth. First the dentist may give you an injection to numb your mouth so you won't feel anything. The tooth is then drilled to remove the decayed part. After that the metal filling is put in.

Looking after your teeth

Now you know how important your teeth are. They need looking after if you are going to keep them until you are old. There is a lot to remember about what is good and what is bad for them. The list opposite will help you.

Caring about your teeth means:

Cutting down on sugar and eating fruit sometimes instead of candy.
Eating crunchy foods like apples, nuts, and raw carrots.
Cleaning your teeth properly at least twice a day and especially before going to bed, using a fluoride toothpaste.
Using disclosing tablets and a fluoride mouthwash.
Going to the dentist every six months.

Not caring about your teeth means:

Eating too many foods with sugar in them like candy, chocolate, cake, jam, cookies, and ice-cream.
Using a worn-out old toothbrush.
Cleaning your teeth in ten seconds flat.
Not going to the dentist.

Word list

Blood vessels The tubes that carry blood around your body.
Brace Wire bands fitted onto the teeth to help straighten them.
Canine teeth The sharp-pointed teeth next to the incisors.
Dentin A material, harder than bone, that makes up most of the tooth.
Enamel The hard, white covering of a tooth.
Fluoride A chemical that strengthens tooth enamel.
Filling Metal that a dentist puts into a tooth cavity.
Gums The firm, pink flesh around your teeth.
Incisors The sharp front teeth between the canines.
Molars The flat, bumpy back teeth.
Nerves The "wires" that carry messages to and from your brain.
Plaque A sticky film that clings to teeth.
Teething When baby teeth push through the gums.
X ray A photograph taken by powerful rays that can pass through most things except metal and bone.

Index

Adult teeth 8–9

Baby teeth 6–7, 8, 9
Bacteria 15
Braces 21, 24

Canines 12, 24
Cleaning teeth 16–19, 23

Decay 14–15
Dentin 11, 24
Dentist 15, 20, 21, 23
Disclosing tablets 17, 23

Enamel 11, 17

Filling 21, 24
Fluoride 17, 23, 24

Gums 4, 7, 8, 10, 24

Incisors 12, 24

Jawbones 7, 10

Losing teeth 6–9

Molars 12, 24

Nerves 11, 24

Plaque 15, 17, 24

Saliva 13
Sugar 14, 15, 23

Teething 7
Toothache 11
Toothbrush 16
Tooth fairy 9

X ray 20, 24